D0445189

MOTHER GOOSE

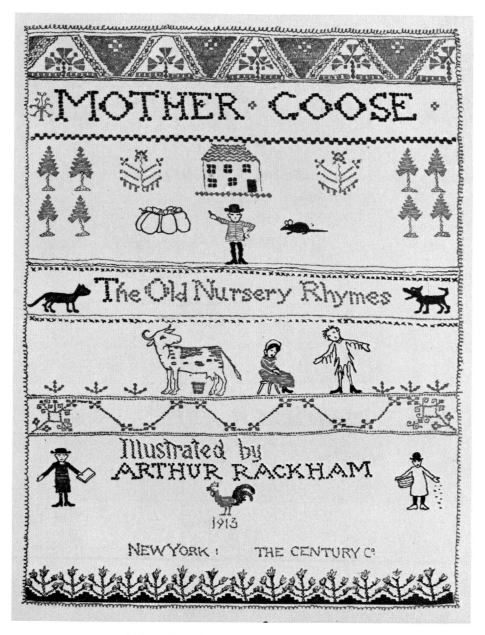

TITLE PAGE FROM ORIGINAL EDITION.

MOTHER GOOSE
The Old Nursery Rhymes

Illustrated by
ARTHUR RACKHAM

WEATHERVANE BOOKS
NEW YORK

FOREWORD TO THE 1978 EDITION

The largest gravestone in Old Boston's Granary bears the name of Mother Goose. This will surprise many who thought that Mother Goose was no more corporeal than Uncle Sam or John Bull. Buried beneath the monument is one Elizabeth Goose, or Vergoose, the mother-in-law of Thomas Fleet, printer. In 1860 a claim was advanced that Mr. Fleet had published in 1719 in Boston *Songs for the Nursery, or, Mother Goose's Melodies*, an anthology compiled by Mrs. Goose. As satisfying as this sounds, it is very probably untrue, as bibliographers have for about seventy-five years agreed that the collection was first published in London in 1760, and that it was based on English and French sources, including Charles Perrault's *Comptes de ma mere d'oye (Tales of Mother Goose)*, published in 1697. Thus, the true identity of Mother Goose remains, at best, slippery.

Arthur Rackham selected these poems in 1913, using the versions he himself knew as a child. We will all recognize them, though, for they differ only slightly from the versions our mothers repeated to us. His illustrations make the rhymes even more vivid. Although most of the rhymes tell simple stories, Rackham's visualizations are complex. Look, for example, at the color plates for "Hey! diddle diddle" and "As I was going to St. Ives," where the detail is complete, and the dream-like quality of the poems is amazingly well captured. Rackham, the foremost book illustrator of Edwardian England, here displays the sophistication of an adult's eye and the exuberance of a child's imagination.

SOLOMON J. SCHEPPS
New York City, October, 1978

Special material copyright © MCMLXXVIII by Crown Publishers, Inc.
All rights reserved.
This edition is published by Weathervane Books, distributed by Crown Publishers, Inc.
b   c   d   e   f   g   h
WEATHERVANE 1978 PRINTING
Manufactured in the United States of America

Library of Congress Cataloging in Publication Data

Mother Goose.
    Mother Goose.

    Includes index.
    SUMMARY: More than 270 nursery rhymes chosen by the
famous illustrator himself as the ones he loved best in
his childhood.
    1. Nursery rhymes.   [1. Nursery rhymes]
I. Rackham, Arthur, 1867-1939.   II. Title.
PZ8.3.M85Rac   1978   398.8   78-11469
ISBN 0-517-26642-3

INDEX OF FIRST LINES

LIST OF ILLUSTRATIONS

COLORED PLATES

BLACK AND WHITE PICTURES

FOREWORD

There are many more Nursery Rhymes than those in this book, but these are the ones I like best, and I think most of the best known are among them. They are those I loved in my own nursery days, and I have chosen the forms I knew then. I think one may do so, as nursery rhymes have, until recently, been handed on only by oral tradition, with its inevitable variations. At home we never had any complete book of them; most we knew came direct from our elders. The children of the present day have often several printed versions of the same rhyme to choose from, but they do not seem to be confused by them. They make their own selection and go on inventing new variations. And however much they alter and add to our old friend, Mother Goose's original collection, they still use her name.

A. R.

The Nursery Rhymes of Mother Goose
illustrated by Arthur Rackham

Baa, baa, black sheep,
Have you any wool?
Yes, sir, yes, sir,
Three bags full:

One for my master,
And one for my dame,
And one for the little boy
Who lives in our lane.

Bye, baby bunting,
Daddy's gone a-hunting,
To get a little rabbit's skin
To wrap the baby bunting in.

Danty, baby, diddy,
What shall her mummy do wid' e?
  Sit in a lap
  And give her some pap,
Danty, baby, diddy.

Dance, Thumbkin, dance;
(keep the thumb in motion
Dance, ye merrymen, everyone;
(all the fingers in motion
For Thumbkin, he can dance alone,
(the thumb alone moving
Thumbkin, he can dance alone;
(the thumb alone moving

Dance, Foreman, dance,
(the first finger moving
Dance, ye merrymen, everyone;
(all moving
But Foreman, he can dance alone,
(the first finger moving
Foreman, he can dance alone,
(the first finger moving

Dance, Longman, dance,
(the second finger moving
Dance, ye merrymen, everyone;
(all moving

3

For Longman, he can dance alone,
(the second finger moving
Longman, he can dance alone.
(the second finger moving

Dance, Ringman, dance,
(the third finger moving
Dance, ye merrymen, dance;
(all moving
But Ringman cannot dance alone,
(the third finger moving
Ringman, he cannot dance alone.
(the third finger moving

Dance, Littleman, dance,
(the fourth finger moving
Dance, ye merrymen, dance,
(all moving
But Littleman, he can dance alone,
(the fourth finger moving
Littleman, he can dance alone.
(the fourth finger moving

Ding, dong, bell,
Pussy's in the well!
Who put her in?
Little Tommy Green.
Who pulled her out?—
Litte Johnny Stout.
What a naughty boy was that
To try to drown poor pussy cat,
Who never did any harm,
But killed the mice in his father's barn.

Dance to your daddy,
My little babby;
Dance to your daddy,
My little lamb.

You shall have a fishy,
In a little dishy;
You shall have a fishy
When the boat comes in.

Georgie Porgie, pudding and pie,
Kissed the girls and made them cry;
When the girls come out to play,
Georgie Porgie runs away.

Great A, little A,
This pancake day;
Toss the ball high,
Throw the ball low,
Those that come after
May sing heigh-ho!

Handy-Spandy, Jack-a-dandy,
Loves plum-cake and sugar-candy.
He bought some at a grocer's shop,
And pleased, away he went, hop, hop, hop.

Here's Sulky Sue,
What shall we do?
Turn her face to the wall
Till she comes to.

How many miles is it to Babylon?—
    Threescore miles and ten.
Can I get there by candle-light?—
    Yes, and back again!
If your heels are nimble and light,
You may get there by candle-light.

Hector Protector was dressed all in green;
Hector Protector was sent to the Queen.
The Queen did not like him,
No more did the King:
So Hector Protector was sent back again.

Here we go round the mulberry bush,
The mulberry bush, the mulberry bush,
Here we go round the mulberry bush,
On a cold and frosty morning.

This is the way we wash our hands,
Wash our hands, wash our hands,
This is the way we wash our hands,
On a cold and frosty morning.

This is the way we wash our clothes,
Wash our clothes, wash our clothes,
This is the way we wash our clothes,
On a cold and frosty morning.

This is the way we go to school,
Go to school, go to school,
This is the way we go to school,
On a cold and frosty morning.

This is the way we come out of school,
Come out of school, come out of school,
This is the way we come out of school
On a cold and frosty morning.

Hark, hark,
The dogs do bark,
Beggars are coming to town:
Some in rags,
And some in tags,
And some in velvet gowns.

Hush-a-bye, baby, on the tree top,
When the wind blows, the cradle will rock;
When the bough breaks, the cradle will
    fall,
Down will come baby, and cradle, and all.

Hickory, Dickory, Dock,
The mouse ran up the clock,
The clock struck one,
The mouse ran down,
Hickory, Dickory, Dock.

Here goes my lord
A trot, a trot, a trot, a trot,
Here goes my lady
A canter, a canter, a canter, a canter!
Here goes my young master
Jockey-hitch, Jockey-hitch, Jockey-hitch,
    Jockey-hitch!
Here goes my young miss,
An amble, an amble, an amble, an amble!
The footman lags behind to tipple ale
    and wine,
And goes gallop, a gallop, a gallop, to
    make up his time.

How does my lady's garden grow?
How does my lady's garden grow?
With cockle shells, and silver bells,
    And pretty maids all of a row.

Hey rub-a-dub, ho rub-a-dub, three maids
    in a tub,
    And what do you think was there?
The butcher, the baker, the candlestick-
    maker,
    And all of them gone to the fair.

Here sits the Lord Mayor,   *(forehead)*
    Here sit his two men;   *(eyes)*
Here sits the cock,   *(right cheek)*
    Here sits the hen;   *(left cheek)*
Here sit the little chickens, *(tip of nose)*
    Here they run in;   *(mouth)*
Chinchopper, chinchopper,
    Chinchopper, chin!   *(chuck the chin)*

Humpty Dumpty sat on a wall,
Humpty Dumpty had a great fall;
All the king's horses and all the king's men
Cannot set Humpty Dumpty up again.

Hey! diddle, diddle,
The cat and the fiddle,
The cow jumped over the moon;
The little dog laughed
To see such sport,
And the dish ran away with the spoon.

How many days has my bab[y]
 Saturday, Sunday, Monday,
Tuesday, Wednesday, Thursday,
 Saturday, Sunday, Monday.

I love little pussy, her coat is so warm,
And if I don't hurt her she'll do me no harm;
So I'll not pull her tail, nor drive her away,
But pussy and I very gently will play.

to play?

Friday,

I went up ... pair of stairs,
Just like me.
I went up two pair of stairs.
2 Just like me.
1 I went into a room.
2 Just like me.
1 I looked out of the window.
2 Just like me.
1 And there I saw a monkey.
2 Just like me.

I won't be my father's Jack,
    I won't be my mother's Gill,
I will be the fiddler's wife,
    And have music when I will.
T'other little tune,
T'other little tune,
Pr'ythee, love, play me
T'other little tune.

Jack Sprat
Had a cat,
It had but one ear;
    It went to buy butter
When butter was dear.

Jack and Jill went up the hill,
    To fetch a pail of water;
Jack fell down, and broke his crown,
    And Jill came tumbling after.

Then up Jack got and home did trot
    As fast as he could caper,
And went to bed to mend his head
    With vinegar and brown paper.

Johnny shall have a new bonnet,
    And Johnny shall go to the fair,
And Johnny shall have a blue ribbon
    To tie up his bonny brown hair.

And why may not I love Johnny?
    And why may not Johnny love me?
And why may not I love Johnny
    As well as another body?

And here's a leg for a stocking,
    And here is a leg for a shoe,
And he has a kiss for his daddy,
    And two for his mammy, I trow.

And why may not I love Johnny?
    And why may not Johnny love me?
And why may not I love Johnny,
    As well as another body?

Little Bo-peep has lost her sheep,
    And can't tell where to find them;
Leave them alone, and they'll come home,
    And bring their tails behind them.

Little Bo-peep fell fast asleep,
    And dreamt she heard them bleating;
But when she awoke, she found it a joke,
    For still they were all fleeting.

Then up she took her little crook,
    Determined for to find them;
She found them, indeed, but it made her
        heart bleed,
    For they'd left all their tails behind 'em.

Little Tom Tucker
    Sang for his supper;
What shall he eat?
    White bread and butter.
How shall he cut it
    Without e'er a knife?
How shall he marry
    Without e'er a wife?

Little Jack Horner
Sat in a corner,
Eating a Christmas pie;
He put in his thumb,
And pulled out a plum,
And said, "What a good boy am I!"

Little Betty Blue
Lost her holiday shoe.
What shall little Betty do?
Buy her another
To match the other,
And then she'll walk in two.

Little Bob Snooks was fond of his books,
And loved by his usher and master;
But naughty Jack Spry, he got a black eye,
And carries his nose in a plaster.

Little Jack-a-Dandy
Wanted sugar candy,
And fairly for it cried;
But little Bill Cook,
Who always read his book,
Shall have a horse to ride.

Little girl, little girl, where have you been?
Gathering roses to give to the queen.
Little girl, little girl, what gave she you?
She gave me a diamond as big as my shoe.

"Lend me thy mare to ride a mile?"
"She is lamed, leaping over a stile."
"Alack! and I must keep the fair!
I'll give thee money for thy mare."
"O, O! say you so?
Money will make the mare to go!"

Little maid, pretty maid, whither goest
      thou?
"Down in the forest to milk my cow."
Shall I go with thee? "No, not now;
When I send for thee, then come thou."

Long legs, crooked thighs,
Little head and no eyes.
            (a pair of tongs)

Little Tommy Tittlemouse
Lived in a little house;
He caught fishes
In other men's ditches.

Lucy Locket lost her pocket,
Kitty Fisher found it;
There was not a penny in it,
But a binding round it.

Little Miss Muffett
Sat on a tuffet,
Eating her curds and whey;
There came a great spider,
And sat down beside her,
And frightened Miss Muffett away.

Mary had a little lamb
　　With fleece as white as snow;
And everywhere that Mary went
　　The lamb was sure to go.

It followed her to school one day;
　　That was against the rule;
It made the children laugh and play
　　To see a lamb at school.

And so the teacher turned it out,
　　But still it lingered near,
And waited patiently about
　　Till Mary did appear.

"Why does the lamb love Mary so?"
　　The eager children cry.
"Why, Mary loves the lamb, you know!"
　　The teacher did reply.

Old Mother Hubbard,
She went to the cupboard,
    To get her poor dog a bone,
But when she came there
The cupboard was bare,
    And so the poor dog had none.

She went to the baker's
    To buy him some bread,
And when she came back
    The poor dog was dead.

        She went to the joiner's
            To buy him a coffin,
        And when she came back
            The poor dog was laughing.

She took a clean dish
    To get him some tripe,
And when she came back
    He was smoking his pipe.

        She went to the ale-house
            To get him some beer,
        And when she came back
            The dog sat in a chair.

She went to the tavern
   For white wine and red,
And when she came back
   The dog stood on his head.

      She went to the hatter's
         To buy him a hat,
      And when she came back
         He was feeding the cat.

She went to the barber's
   To buy him a wig,
And when she came back
   He was dancing a jig.

      She went to the fruiterer's
         To buy him some fruit,
      And when she came back
         He was playing the flute.

She went to the tailor's
   To buy him a coat,
And when she came back
   He was riding a goat.

She went to the cobbler's
  To buy him some shoes,
And when she came back
  He was reading the news.

She went to the seamstress
  To buy him some linen,
And when she came back
  The dog was spinning.

She went to the hosier's
  To buy him some hose,
And when she came back
  He was dressed in his clothes.

The dame made a courtesy,
  The dog made a bow;
The dame said, "Your servant,"
  The dog said, "Bow, wow!"

One, two,
Buckle my shoe;
Three, four,
Knock at the door;
Five, six,
Pick up sticks;
Seven, eight,
Lay them straight;
Nine, ten,
A good fat hen;
Eleven, twelve,
Dig and delve;
Thirteen, fourteen,
Maids a-courting;
Fifteen, sixteen,
Maids in the kitchen;
Seventeen, eighteen,
Maids a-waiting;
Nineteen, twenty,
My plate's empty.

Pat-a-cake, pat-a-cake, baker's man!
Make me a cake as fast as you can:
Prick it, and stick it, and mark it with B,
And put it in the oven for Baby and me.

Rock-a-bye, baby, thy cradle is green;
Father's a nobleman, mother's a queen;
And Betty's a lady, and wears a gold
    ring;
And Johnny's a drummer, and drums for
    the king.

    Rub-a-dub-dub,
      Three men in a tub;
    And who do you think they be?
      The butcher, the baker,
      The candlestick-maker;
Turn 'em out, knaves all three!

Ride a cock-horse to Banbury Cross,
To see a fine lady upon a white horse,
With rings on her fingers, and bells on her
    toes,
She shall have music wherever she goes.

Rabbit, Rabbit, Rabbit Pie!
Come, my ladies, come and buy;
Else your babies they will cry.

Ride away, ride away, Johnny shall ride,
And he shall have pussy cat tied to one
    side;
And he shall have little dog tied to the
    other;
And Johnny shall ride to see his grand-
    mother.

Robin the Bobbin, the big bouncing Ben,
He ate more meat than fourscore men;
He ate a cow, he ate a calf,
He ate a butcher and a half;
He ate a church, he ate a steeple,
He ate the priest and all the people!

See, see! what shall I see?
A horse's head where his tail should be.

Shoe the horse, and shoe the mare;
But let the little colt go bare.

See-saw, Margery Daw,
Johnny shall have a new master;
He shall have but a penny a day,
Because he can't work any faster.

See-saw, sacaradown,
Which is the way to London town?
One foot up, and the other foot down,
And that is the way to London town.

There was an old woman who lived in a shoe;
She had so many children she didn't know
        what to do;
She gave them some broth without any bread,
She whipped them all round, and sent them
        to bed.

To market, to market, to buy a fat pig,
Home again, home again, dancing a jig.
To market, to market, to buy a fat hog,
Home again, home again, jiggety jog.

This little pig went
to market;

This little pig stayed at home;

This little pig had
roast beef;

"BYE, BABY BUNTING."

"HARK, HARK, THE DOGS DO BARK!"

"HEY! DIDDLE, DIDDLE, THE CAT AND THE FIDDLE!"

"JACK AND JILL."

This little pig had none;

This little pig said,
wee, wee, wee!
All the way home.

To market, to market,
To buy a plum bun,
Home again, home again,
Market is done.

"To bed, to bed," says Sleepy-head.
"Let's stay awhile," says Slow;
"Put on the pot," says Greedy-gut,
"We'll sup before we go."

To market ride the gentlemen,
    So do we, so do we;
Then comes the country clown,
    Hobbledy gee, Hobbledy gee;
First go the ladies, nim, nim, nim;
Next come the gentlemen, trim, trim,
    trim;
Then come the country clowns, gallop-
    a-trot.

There were two blackbirds
   Sitting on a hill,
The one named Jack,
   And the other named Jill;
Fly away, Jack!
Fly away, Jill!
Come again, Jack!
Come again, Jill!

1 This pig went to the barn;
2 This ate all the corn;
3 This said he would tell;
4 This said he wasn't well;
5 This went week, week, week, over
     the door-sill.

This is the way the ladies
ride,
Tri, tre, tre, tree,
Tri, tre, tre, tree!
This is the way the ladies
ride,
Tri, tre, tre, tre, tri-tre-
tre-tree!

This is the way
the gentlemen ride,
Gallop-a-trot,
Gallop-a-trot!
This is the way
the gentlemen ride,
Gallop-a-gallop-a-trot!

This is the way the farmers
ride,
Hobbledy-hoy,
Hobbledy-hoy!
This is the way the farmers
ride,
Hobbledy hobbledy-hoy!

There was an old woman had three sons,
Jerry and James and John:
Jerry was hung, James was drowned,
John was lost, and never was found;
And there was an end of her three sons,
Jerry and James and John!

A farmer went trotting
    Upon his grey mare,
    Bumpety, bumpety, bump!
With his daughter behind him
    So rosy and fair,
    Lumpety, lumpety, lump!

A raven cried "Croak!"
    And they all tumbled down,
    Bumpety, bumpety, bump!
The mare broke her knees,
    And the farmer his crown,
    Lumpety, lumpety, lump!

The mischievous raven flew
    Laughing away,
    Bumpety, bumpety, bump!
And vowed he would serve them
    The same the next day,
    Lumpety, lumpety, lump!

A, apple-pie;

B bit it;

C cut it;

D dealt it;

E ate it;

F fought for it;

G got it;

H had it;

J joined it;

K kept it;

L longed for it;

M mourned for it;

N nodded at it;

O opened it;

P peeped in it;   V viewed it;

Q quartered it;   W wanted it;

R ran for it;   X, Y, and Z

S stole it;   and Amperse—and
                All wished for a
T took it;   piece in hand.

A was an archer, and shot at a frog,

B was a butcher, and had a great dog.

C was a captain, all covered with lace,

D was a drunkard, and had a red face.

E was an esquire, with pride on his
brow,

F was a farmer, and followed the
plough.

G was a gamester, who had but ill luck,

H was a hunter, and hunted a buck.

I was an innkeeper, who loved to
    bouse,

J was a joiner, and built up a house.

K was King William, who once governed
    this land,

L was a lady, who had a white hand.

M was a miser, and hoarded up gold,

N was a nobleman, gallant and bold.

O was an oyster wench, and went about town,

P was a parson, and wore a black gown.

Q was a queen, who was fond of good flip,

R was a robber, and wanted a whip.

S was a sailor, and spent all he got,

T was a tinker, and mended a pot.

U was an usurer, a miserable elf,

V was a vintner, who drank all himself.

W was a watchman, and guarded the
door,

X was expensive, and so became poor,

Y was a youth, that did not love school,

Z was a zany, a poor harmless fool.

A curious discourse about an Apple-pie,
that passed between the Twenty-Five
letters at Dinner-time.

Says A, Give me a good large slice.

Says B, A little Bit, but nice.

Says C, Cut me a piece of Crust.

Says D, It is as Dry as Dust.

Says E, I'll Eat now, fast who will.

Says F, I vow I'll have my Fill.

Says G, Give it to me Good and Great.

Says H, A little bit I Hate.

Says I, I love the Juice the best.

And K the very same confessed.

Says L, There's nothing more I Love.

Says M, It makes your teeth to Move.

N Noticed what the others said.

O Others' plates with grief sur-
veyed.

P Praised the cook up to the life.

Q Quarelled 'cause he'd a bad
knife.

Says R, It Runs short, I'm afraid.

S Silent set, and nothing said.

T Thought that Talking might lose time.

U Understood it at meals a crime.

W Wished there had been a quince in.

Says X, Those cooks there's no con-vincing.

A diller, a dollar,
A ten o'clock scholar,
What makes you come so soon?
You used to come at ten o'clock,
But now you come at noon.

A, B, C, tumble down D,
The cat's in the cupboard, and can't
    see me.

A long-tailed pig, and a short-tailed pig,
Or a pig without e'er a tail,
A sow pig, or a boar pig,
Or a pig with a curly tail.

An apple pie, when it looks nice,
Would make one long to have a slice,
But if the taste should prove so, too,
I fear one slice would scarcely do.
So to prevent my asking twice,
Pray, mamma, cut a good large slice.

A pie sate on a pear-tree,
A pie sate on a pear-tree,
A pie sate on a pear-tree,
Heigh O, heigh O, heigh O!
Once so merrily hopped she,
Twice so merrily hopped she,
Thrice so merrily hopped she,
Heigh O, heigh O, heigh O!

Apple-pie, pudding, and pancake,
All begins with A.

Around the green gravel the grass grows
    green,
And all the pretty maids are plain to be
    seen;
Wash them with milk, and clothe them
    with silk,
And write their names with a pen and ink.

As I was going to sell my eggs
I met a man with bandy legs;
Bandy legs and crooked toes,
I tripped up his heels, and he fell on his
    nose.

As little Jenny Wren
    Was sitting by the shed,
She waggled with her tail,
    And nodded with her head.
She waggled with her tail,
    And nodded with her head,
As little Jenny Wren
    Was sitting by the shed.

As soft as silk, as white as milk,
As bitter as gall, a strong wall,
And a green coat covers me all.

(a walnut)

Bat, bat,
Come under my hat,
And I'll give you a slice of bacon;
And when I bake,
I'll give you a cake,
If I am not mistaken.

Bessy Bell and Mary Gray,
    They were two bonny lasses;
They built their house upon the lea,
    And covered it with rashes.

Bessy kept the garden gate,
    And Mary kept the pantry:
Bessy always had to wait,
    While Mary lived in plenty.

"Billy, Billy, come and play,
While the sun shines bright as day."

"Yes, my Polly, so I will,
For I love to please you still."

"Billy, Billy, have you seen
Sam and Betsy on the green?"

"Yes, my Poll, I saw them pass,
Skipping o'er the new-mown grass."

"Billy, Billy, come along,
And I will sing a pretty song."

Bless you, bless you, burny-bee;
Say, when will your wedding be?
If it be to-morrow day,
Take your wings and fly away.

Bow, wow, says the dog;
Mew, mew, says the cat;
Grunt, grunt, goes the hog;
And squeak goes the rat.

Chirp, chirp, says the sparrow;
Caw, caw, says the crow;
Quack, quack, says the duck;
And what cuckoos say, you know.

So, with sparrows and cuckoos;
With rats and with dogs;
With ducks and with crows;
With cats and with hogs.

A fine song I have made,
To please you, my dear;
And if it's well sung,
'Twill be charming to hear.

Barber, barber, shave a pig;
How many hairs will make a wig?
"Four-and-twenty, that's enough,"
Give the poor barber a pinch of snuff.

Come when your called,
Do what you're bid,
Shut the door after you,
Never be chid.

Cross Patch,
Draw the latch,
Sit by the fire and spin;
Take a cup,
And drink it up,
Then call your neighbors in.

Cock a doodle doo!
My dame has lost her shoe;
My master's lost his fiddling stick,
And don't know what to do.

Cock a doodle doo!
What is my dame to do?
Till master finds his fiddling stick,
She'll dance without her shoe.

Cock a doodle doo!
Dame has lost her shoe;

Gone to bed and scratched her head,
And can't tell what to do.

Cock a doodle doo!
My dame has lost her shoe,
And master's found his fiddling stick,
Sing doodle doodle doo!

Cock a doodle doo!
My dame will dance with you.
While master fiddles his fiddling stick,
For dame and doodle doo.

Curly locks! curly locks! wilt thou be
mine!
Thou shalt not wash dishes, nor yet feed
the swine;
But sit on a cushion and sew a fine seam,
And feed upon strawberries, sugar, and
cream!

Cry, baby, cry,
Put your finger in your eye,
And tell your mother it wasn't I.

Diddle-ty—diddle-ty—dumpty,
The cat ran up the plum-tree,
Half-a-crown
To fetch her down,
Diddle-ty—diddle-ty—dumpty.

Deedle, deedle dumpling, my son John,
Went to bed with his trousers on,
One shoe off, and the other shoe on;
Deedle, deedle dumpling, my son John.

Daffy-Down-Dilly has come up to town,
In a yellow petticoat, and a green gown.

Elizabeth, Elspeth, Betsy, and Bess,
They all went together to seek a bird's nest,
They found a bird's nest with five eggs in,
They all took one, and left four in.

Fiddle-de-dee, fiddle-de-dee,
The fly shall marry the bumble-bee.
They went to church, and married was she:
The fly has married the bumble-bee.

Girls and boys, come out to play,
The moon doth shine as bright as day;
Leave your supper, and leave your sleep,
And come with your playfellows into the
      street.
Come with a whoop, come with a call,
Come with a good will or come not at all.
Up the ladder and down the wall,
A halfpenny roll will serve us all.
You find milk, and I'll find flour,
And we'll have a pudding in half-an-hour.

Great A, little A,
Bouncing B,
The cat's in the cupboard,
And can't see me.

Goosey, goosey, gander,
Whither shall I wander?
Upstairs and downstairs,
And in my lady's chamber.

There I met an old man
That wouldn't say his prayers;
I took him by the left leg,
And threw him downstairs.

Gay go up and gay go down,
To ring the bells of London town.

Oranges and lemons,
Say the bells of St. Clement's.

You owe me ten shillings,
Say the bells of St. Helen's.

When will you pay me?
Say the bells of Old Bailey.

When I grow rich,
Say the bells of Shoreditch.

Pray when will that be?
Say the bells of Stepney.

I am sure I don't know,
Says the great bell of Bow.

Brickbats and tiles,
Say the bells of St. Giles'.

Halfpence and farthings,
Say the bells of St. Martin's.

Pancakes and fritters,
Say the bells of St. Peter's.

Two sticks and an apple,
Say the bells of Whitechapel.

Old Father Baldpate,
Say the slow bells of Aldgate.

Poker and tongs,
Say the bells of St. John's.

Kettles and pans,
Say the bells of St. Ann's.

Hot-cross Buns!
Old woman runs!
One a penny, two a penny,
Hot-cross Buns!

If ye have no daughters,
Give them to your sons.
One a penny, two a penny,
Hot-cross Buns!

Here am I, little jumping Joan,
When nobody's with me,
I'm always alone.

Hickety, pickety, my black hen,
She lays eggs for gentlemen;
Gentlemen come every day
To see what my black hen doth lay.

I'll tell you a story
About Jack a Nory,—
And now my story's begun;
I'll tell you another
About Jack his brother,—
And now my story's done.

I am a gold lock.
I am a gold key.
I am a silver lock.
I am a silver key.
I am a brass lock.
I am a brass key.
I am a lead lock.
I am a lead key.
I am a monk lock.
I am a monk key!

I had a little moppet,
I kept it in my pocket,
And fed it with corn and hay,
There came a proud beggar,
Who swore he would have her,
And stole little moppet away.

If a man who turnips cries,
Cries not when his father dies,
It is proof that he would rather
Have a turnip than his father.

If wishes were horses,
  Beggars might ride;
If turnips were watches,
  I would wear one by my side.

I had a little hen, the prettiest ever seen,
She washed up the dishes, and kept the
    house clean;
She went to the mill to fetch me some
    flour,
She brought it home in less than an hour;
She baked me my bread, she brewed me
    my ale,
She sat by the fire and told me a fine tale.

I had a little nut tree, nothing would it
    bear
But a silver apple and a golden pear;
The King of Spain's daughter came to
    see me,
And all for the sake of my little nut tree.

I skipped over water, I danced over sea,
And all the birds in the air couldn't
    catch me.

I will sing you a song,
Though 'tis not very long,
Of the woodcock and the sparrow,
Of the little dog that burned his tail,
And he shall be whipped to-morrow.

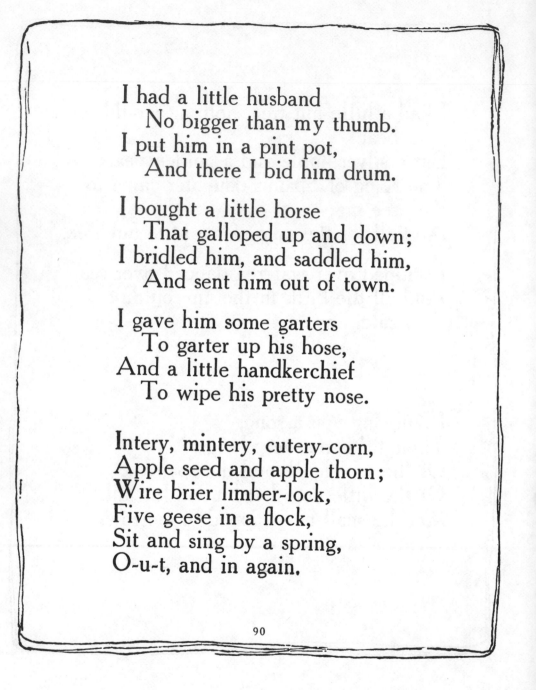

I had a little husband
   No bigger than my thumb.
I put him in a pint pot,
   And there I bid him drum.

I bought a little horse
   That galloped up and down;
I bridled him, and saddled him,
   And sent him out of town.

I gave him some garters
   To garter up his hose,
And a little handkerchief
   To wipe his pretty nose.

Intery, mintery, cutery-corn,
Apple seed and apple thorn;
Wire brier limber-lock,
Five geese in a flock,
Sit and sing by a spring,
O-u-t, and in again.

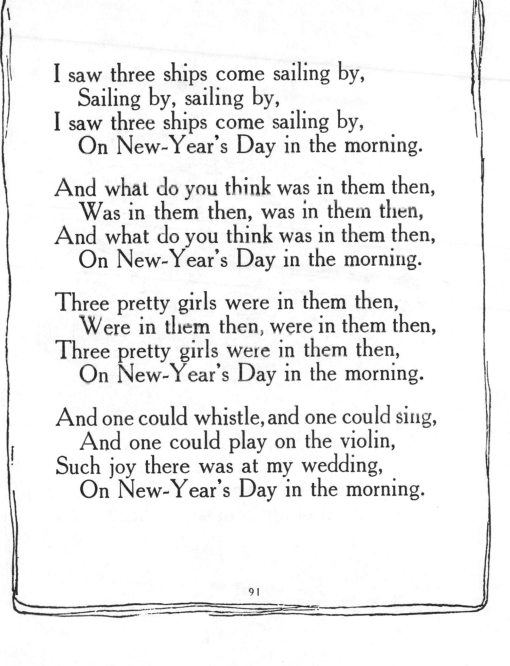

I saw three ships come sailing by,
    Sailing by, sailing by,
I saw three ships come sailing by,
    On New-Year's Day in the morning.

And what do you think was in them then,
    Was in them then, was in them then,
And what do you think was in them then,
    On New-Year's Day in the morning.

Three pretty girls were in them then,
    Were in them then, were in them then,
Three pretty girls were in them then,
    On New-Year's Day in the morning.

And one could whistle, and one could sing,
    And one could play on the violin,
Such joy there was at my wedding,
    On New-Year's Day in the morning.

I saw a ship a-sailing,
A-sailing on the sea;
And, oh! it was all laden
With pretty things for thee?

There were comfits in the cabin,
And apples in the hold;
The sails were all of silk,
And the masts were made of gold.

The four-and-twenty sailors
That stood between the decks,
Were four-and-twenty white mice
With chains about their necks.

The captain was a duck,
With a packet on his back;
And when the ship began to move,
The captain said, "Quack! Quack!"

Jack Sprat could eat no fat,
His wife could eat no lean,
And so, betwixt them both,
They licked the platter clean.

Jeanie, come tie my,
Jeanie, come tie my,
Jeanie, come tie my bonnie cravat;
I've tied it behind,
I've tied it before,
And I've tied it so often, I'll tie it no
more.

Jocky was a piper's son,
And he fell in love when he was young,
And the only tune he could play
Was, "Over the hills and far away;"
Over the hills and a great way off,
And the wind will blow my top-knot off.

John Cook had a little grey mare;
   He, haw, hum!
Her back stood up, and her bones they
     were bare;
   He, haw, hum!

John Cook was riding up Shuter's bank;
   He, haw, hum!
And there his nag did kick and prank;
   He, haw, hum!

John Cook was riding up Shuter's hill;
   He, haw, hum!
His mare fell down, and she made her will;
   He, haw, hum!

The bridle and saddle were laid on the
     shelf;
   He, haw, hum;
If you want any more you may sing it
     yourself;
   He, haw, hum!

Jack be nimble,
Jack be quick,
Jack jump over the candlestick.

Lady bird, lady bird, fly away home,
Your house is on fire, your children all gone,
All but one, and her name is Ann,
And she crept under the pudding-pan.

Little Tee Wee,
He went to sea,
In an open boat;
And while afloat
The little boat bended,
And my story's ended.

Love your own, kiss your own,
  Love your own mother, hinny,
For if she was dead and gone,
  You'd ne'er get such another, hinny.

Little Nancy Etticoat,
In a white petticoat,
And a red nose.
The longer she stands,
The shorter she grows.

Little Boy Blue, come blow your horn,
The sheep's in the meadow, the cow's in
    the corn;
Where's the little boy that looks after the
    sheep?
He's under the hay-cock fast asleep.
Will you wake him?   No, not I;
For if I do, he'll be sure to cry.

Little Polly Flinders,
Sat among the cinders,
Warming her pretty little toes;
Her mother came and caught her,
And whipped her little daughter,
For spoiling her nice new clothes.

Mary, Mary,
Quite contrary,
How does your garden grow?
With silver-bells,
And cockle-shells,
And pretty maids all in a row.

Matthew, Mark, Luke and John,
Bless the bed that I lie on.
Four corners to my bed,
Four angels over head,
One to sing and one to pray,
And two to bear my soul away.

Mrs. Bond she went down to the pond in
    a rage,
With plenty of onions, and plenty of sage;
She cried, "Come, little wag-tails, come
    and be killed,
For you shall be stuffed, and my custo-
    mers filled!"

Multiplication is vexation,
    Division is as bad;
The Rule of Three doth puzzle me,
    And Practice drives me mad.

My little old man and I fell out,
I'll tell you what 'twas all about:
I had money and he had none,
And that's the way the row begun.

Master I have, and I am his man,
    Gallop a dreary dun;
Master I have, and I am his man,
    And I'll get a wife as fast I can;
With a heighty gaily gamberally,
    Higgledy, piggledy, niggledy, niggledy,
    Gallop a dreary dun.

Nose, nose, jolly red nose;
And what gave thee that jolly red nose?
Nutmegs and cinnamon, spices and cloves,
And they gave me this jolly red nose.

Now what do you think
    Of little Jack Jingle?
Before he was married
    He used to live single.

Old woman, old woman, shall we go a
    shearing?
"Speak a little louder, sir, I am very
    thick of hearing."
Old woman, old woman, shall I love
    you dearly?
"Thank you, kind sir, I hear you very
    clearly."

Once I saw a little bird
    Come hop, hop, hop;
So I cried, "Little bird,
    Will you stop, stop, stop?"
And was going to the window
    To say, "How do you do?"
But he shook his little tail,
    And far away he flew.

Old mother Twitchett had but one eye,
And a long tail which she let fly;
And every time she went over a gap,
She left a bit of her tail in a trap.

Over the water, and over the sea,
And over the water to Charley.
Charley loves good ale and wine,
And Charley loves good brandy,
And Charley loves a pretty girl,
As sweet as sugar-candy.

Over the water, and over the sea,
And over the water to Charley,
I'll have none of your nasty beef,
Nor I'll have none of your barley;
But I'll have some of your very best flour,
To make a white cake for my Charley.

One, two, three, four, five,
Catching fishes all alive,
Why did you let them go?
Because they bit my finger so.
Which finger did they bite?
The little finger on the right.

Peter Piper picked a peck of pickled
    pepper;
A peck of pickled pepper Peter Piper
    picked;
If Peter Piper picked a peck of pickled
    pepper,
Where's the peck of pickled pepper Peter
    Piper picked?

Polly, put the kettle on,
Polly, put the kettle on,
Polly, put the kettle on,
   And we'll all have tea.

Sukey, take it off again,
Sukey, take it off again,
Sukey, take it off again,
   They're all gone away.

Pussy-cat, pussy-cat, with a white foot,
When is your wedding? for I'll come to't.
The beer's to brew, the bread's to bake,
Pussy-cat, pussy-cat, don't be too late.

Pussy-cat Mole
Jumped over a coal,
And in her best petticoat burnt a great
    hole.
Poor pussy's weeping, she'll have no
    more milk,
Until her best petticoat's mended with
    silk.

Pussy-cat, pussy-cat, where have you been?
I've been up to London to look at the
queen,
Pussy-cat, pussy-cat, what did you there?
I frightened a little mouse under the chair.

"LITTLE MISS MUFFETT."

JACK SPRAT AND HIS WIFE.

"RAIN, RAIN, GO AWAY!"

"THERE WAS AN OLD WOMAN LIVED UNDER A HILL."

Rain, rain, go to Spain,
Don't come back again!

Rowley, Powley, pudding and pie,
Kissed the girls and made them cry;
When the girls began to cry,
Rowley, Powley runs away.

Snail, snail, come out of your hole,
Or else I'll beat you as black as a coal.

Snail, snail, put out your horns,
Here comes a thief to pull down your
    walls.

Rain, rain, go away,
Come again another day;
Little (*Arthur*) wants to play.

An old woman was sweeping her house,
and she found a little crooked sixpence.

"What," said she, "shall I do with this
little sixpence? I will go to market,
and buy a little pig."

As she was coming home, she came
to a stile; but the pig would not go
over the stile.

She went a little farther, and she met a dog.
So she said to the dog—

"Dog, dog, bite pig!
Pig won't get over the stile;
And I shan't get home to-night."

But the dog would not.

She went a little farther, and she met a
stick.   So she said—

"Stick, stick, beat dog!
Dog won't bite pig;
Pig won't get over the stile;
And I shan't get home to-night."

But the stick would not

She went a little farther, and she met a
fire.   So she said—

"Fire, fire, burn stick!
Stick won't beat dog;
Dog won't bite pig;
Pig won't get over the stile;
And I shan't get home to-night."

But the fire would not.

She went a little farther, and she met some
water.   So she said—

"Water, water, quench fire!
Fire won't burn stick;
Stick won't beat dog;
Dog won't bite pig;
Pig won't get over the stile;
And I shan't get home to-night."

But the water would not.

She went a little farther and she met an
ox.   So she said—

"Ox, ox, drink water!
Water won't quench fire;
Fire won't burn stick;
Stick won't beat dog;
Dog won't bite pig;
Pig won't get over the stile;
And I shan't get home to-night."

But the ox would not.

She went a little farther and she met a
butcher.   So she said—

"Butcher, butcher, kill ox!
Ox won't drink water;
Water won't quench fire;
Fire won't burn stick;
Stick won't beat dog;
Dog won't bite pig;
Pig won't get over the stile;
And I shan't get home to-night."

But the butcher would not.

She went a little farther and she met a
rope.   So she said—

"Rope, rope, hang butcher!
Butcher won't kill ox;
Ox won't drink water;
Water won't quench fire;
Fire won't burn stick;
Stick won't beat dog;
Dog won't bite pig;
Pig won't get over the stile;
And I shan't get home to-
night."

But the rope would not.

She went a little farther and she met a
rat.   So she said—

Rat, rat, gnaw rope!
Rope won't hang butcher;
Butcher won't kill ox;
Ox won't drink water;
Water won't quench fire;
Fire won't burn stick;
Stick won't beat dog;
Dog won't bite pig;
Pig won't get over the stile;
And I shan't get home to-night."

But the rat would not.

She went a little farther and she met a cat. So she said—

"Cat, cat, kill rat;
Rat won't gnaw rope;
Rope won't hang butcher;
Butcher won't kill ox;
Ox won't drink water;
Water won't quench fire;

Fire won't burn stick;
Stick won't beat dog;
Dog won't bite pig;
Pig won't get over the stile;
And I shan't get home to-night."

The cat said, "If you will give me a saucer
of milk, I will kill the rat."
So the old woman gave the cat the milk,
and when she had lapped up the
milk —

The cat began to kill the rat;

The rat began to gnaw the rope;

The rope began to hang the butcher;

The butcher began to kill the ox;

The ox began to drink the water;

The water began to quench the fire;

The fire began to burn the stick;

The stick began to beat the dog;

The dog began to bite the pig;

The pig jumped over the stile;

And so the old woman got home that
night.

Simple Simon met a pieman,
  Going to the fair;
Says Simple Simon to the pieman,
  "Let me taste your ware."

Says the pieman to Simple Simon,
  "Shoe me first your penny,"
Says Simple Simon to the pieman,
  "Indeed, I have not any."

Simple Simon went a-fishing,
  For to catch a whale;
All the water he had got
  Was in his mother's pail.

Sing a song of sixpence,
  A pocket full of rye;
Four and twenty blackbirds
  Baked in a pie.

When the pie was opened
  The birds began to sing;
Was not that a dainty dish
  To set before the King?

The King was in the counting-house
  Counting out his money;
The Queen was in the parlour
  Eating bread and honey.

The maid was in the garden
  Hanging out the clothes,
Down came a blackbird
  And snapped off her nose.

Sing, sing, what shall I sing?
The cat's run off with the pudding-bag
    string!
Do, do, what shall I do?
The cat has bitten it quite in two.

There was a little boy and a little girl
    Lived in an alley;
Says the little boy to the little girl,
    "Shall I, oh! shall I?"

Says the little girl to the little boy,
    "What shall we do?"
Says the little boy to the little girl,
    "I will kiss you."

The cock's on the housetop blowing his
    horn;
The bull's in the barn a-threshing of corn;
The maids in the meadows are making of
    hay;
The ducks in the river are swimming
    away.

    The cuckoo's a fine bird,
      He sings as he flies;
    He brings us good tidings,
      He tells us no lies.

    He sucks little birds' eggs,
      To make his voice clear;
    And when he sings "cuckoo!"
      The summer is near.

The dove says coo, coo, what shall I do?
I can scarce maintain two.
Pooh, pooh! says the wren, I have got ten,
And keep them all like gentlemen!

The King of France went up the hill,
    With twenty thousand men;
The King of France came down the hill,
    And ne'er went up again.

The man in the moon,
Came down too soon,
To inquire his way to Norwich.
He went by the south,
And burnt his mouth
With eating cold plum-porridge.

There was a man of our town,
And he was wondrous wise;
He jumped into a quickset hedge,
And scratched our both his eyes:
And when he saw his eyes were out,
With all his might and main
He jumped into another hedge,
And scratched 'em in again.

There was a man, and he had naught,
  And robbers came to rob him;
He crept up to the chimney pot,
  And then they thought they had him.

But he got down on t'other side,
  And then they could not find him;
He ran fourteen miles in fifteen days,
  And never looked behind him.

The rose is red, the violet blue,
The gilly-flower sweet, and so are you.
These are the words you bade me say
For a pair of new gloves on Easter-day.

The winds they did blow,
    The leaves they did wag;
Along came a beggar-boy,
    And put me in his bag.

He took me up to London,
    A lady did me buy;
Put me in a silver cage,
    And hung me up on high.

With apples by the fire,
    And nuts for to crack;
Besides a little feather-bed,
    To rest my little back.

There was an old woman lived under a
    hill,
And if she's not gone, she lives there still

There was an old woman, her name it
    was Peg,
Her head was of wood, and she wore a
    cork-leg.
The neighbors all pitched her into the
    water,
Her leg was drowned first, and her head
    followed a'ter.

There was an old woman lived under a
    hill,
She put a mouse in a bag and sent it to
    the mill;
The miller did swear by the point of his
    knife,
He never took toll of a mouse in his life.

This is the house that Jack built.

This is the malt
That lay in the house that Jack built.

This is the rat,
That ate the malt
That lay in the house that Jack built.

This is the cat,
That killed the rat,
That ate the malt
That lay in the house that Jack built.

This is the dog,
That worried the cat,
That killed the rat,
That ate the malt
That lay in the house that Jack built.

This is the cow with the crumpled horn,
That tossed the dog,
That worried the cat,
That killed the rat,
That ate the malt
That lay in the house that Jack built.

This is the maiden all forlorn,
That milked the cow with the crumpled
    horn,

That tossed the dog,
That worried the cat,
That killed the rat,
That ate the malt
That lay in the house that Jack built.

This is the man all tattered and torn,
That kissed the maiden all forlorn,
That milked the cow with the crumpled
    horn,
That tossed the dog,
That worried the cat,
That killed the rat,
That ate the malt
That lay in the house that Jack built.

This is the priest all shaven and shorn,
That married the man all tattered and torn,
That kissed the maiden all forlorn,
That milked the cow with the crumpled
        horn,
That tossed the dog,
That worried the cat,
That killed the rat,
That ate the malt
That lay in the house that Jack built.

This is the cock that crowed in the morn,
That waked the priest all shaven and
        shorn,
That married the man all tattered and torn,

That kissed the maiden all forlorn,
That milked the cow with the crumpled
    horn,
That tossed the dog,
That worried the cat,
That killed the rat,
That ate the malt
That lay in the house that Jack built.

This is the farmer sowing the corn,
That kept the cock that crowed in the
    morn,
That waked the priest all shaven and
    shorn,

That married the man all tattered and torn,
That kissed the maiden all forlorn,
That milked the cow with the crumpled
      horn,
That tossed the dog,
That worried the cat,
That killed the rat,
That ate the malt
That lay in the house that Jack built.

Tom, Tom, the piper's son,
Stole a pig, and away he run!
The pig was eat, and Tom was beat,
And Tom went roaring down the street.

Tom, Tom, the piper's son.
He learned to play when he was young,
But all the tunes that he could play,
Was "Over the hills and far away".
Over the hills and a great way off,
And the wind will blow my top-knot off.

Now Tom with his pipe made such a
        noise,
That he pleased both the girls and boys,
And they stopped to hear him play,
"Over the hills and far away".

Tom with his pipe did play with such
        skill,
That those who heard him could never
        keep still;
Wherever they heard they began for to
        dance,
Even pigs on their hind legs would after
        him prance.

As Dolly was milking her cow one day,
Tom took out his pipe and began for to
    play;
So Doll and the cow danced "the
    Cheshire round,"
Till the pail was broke, and the milk
    ran on the ground.

He met old Dame Trot with a basket of
    eggs,
He used his pipe, and she used her legs;
She danced about till the eggs were all
    broke,
She began for to fret, but he laughed at
    the joke.

He saw a cross fellow was beating an ass,
Heavy laden with pots, pans, dishes and
    glass;
He took out his pipe and played them a
    tune,
And the jackass's load was lightened full
    soon.

Three blind mice! Three blind
  mice!
    See how they run! See how
      they run!
They all ran after the farmer's
    wife,
Who cut off their tails with the
    carving knife,
Did you ever see such fun in
    your life?
    As three blind mice.

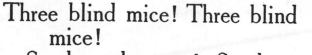

Three little kittens they lost their mittens,
And they began to cry
    Oh! mammy dear,
    We sadly fear
That we have lost our mittens.

    Lost your mittens!
    You naughty kittens!
Then you shall have no pie.
    Mee-ow, mee-ow, mee-ow,
    Mee-ow, mee-ow, mee-ow.

The three little kittens they found their
        mittens,
And they began to cry,
    Oh! mammy dear,
    See here, see here!
See, we have found our mittens.

What, found your mittens,
   You little kittens,
Then you shall have some pie.
   Purr-r, purr-r, purr-r,
   Purr-r, purr-r, purr-r.

The three little kittens put on their
         mittens,
And soon ate up the pie;
   Oh! mother dear,
   We greatly fear,
That we have soiled our mittens.

   Soiled your mittens!
   You naughty kittens!
Then they began to sigh,
   Mi-ew, mi-ew, mi-ew,
   Mi-ew, mi-ew, mi-ew.

The three little kittens they washed their
      mittens,
And hung them up to dry;
  Oh! mammy dear,
  Look here, look here,
  Do you not hear,
That we have washed our mittens?

  Washed your mittens!
  Oh! you're good kittens.
But I smell a rat close by.
  Hush! hush! mee-ow, mee-ow,
  Mee-ow, mee-ow, mee-ow.

The northwind doth blow,
And we shall have snow,
And what will the Robin do then?
  Poor thing!

He'll sit in a barn,
And keep himself warm,
And hide his head under his wing.
  Poor thing!

What are little boys made of?
What are little boys made of?
"Snaps and snails, and puppy-dog's tails;
And that's what little boys are made of."

What are little girls made of?
What are little girls made of?
"Sugar and spice, and all that's nice;
And that's what little girls are made of."

Upon St. Paul's steeple stands a tree,
As full of apples as may be.
The little boys of London town,
They run with hooks and pull them down;
And then they run from hedge to hedge
Until they come to London Bridge.

Who goes here?
"A grenadier.'
What do you want?
"A pot of beer."
Where is your money?
"I've forgot."
Get you gone,
You drunken sot!

When the days begin to lengthen
The cold begins to strengthen.

Wee Willie Winkie runs through the
town,
Upstairs and downstairs in his night-
gown,
Rapping at the window, crying
through the lock,

"Are the children
in their beds, for now
it's eight o'clock?"

Yankee Doodle went to town
Upon a little pony;
He stuck a feather in his hat,
And called it Macaroni.

Yet didn't you see, yet didn't you see,
What naughty tricks they put upon me:
They broke my pitcher,
And spilt my water,
And huffed my mother,
And chid her daughter,
And kissed my sister instead of me.

A sunshiny shower
Won't last half an hour.

A red sky at night,
Is the shepherd's delight.
A red sky in the morning,
Is the shepherd's warning.

"Come, let's to bed,"
Says Sleepy-head;
"Tarry a while", says Slow.
"Put on the pan,"
Says Greedy Nan,
"Let's sup before we go."

A carrion crow sat on an oak,
   Fol de riddle, lol de riddle, hi ding do,
Watching a tailor make his cloak;
   Sing heigh, sing ho, the carrion crow,
   Fol de riddle, lol de riddle, hi ding do.

Wife, bring me my old bent bow,
   Fol de riddle, lol de riddle, hi ding do,
That I may shoot yon carrion crow;
   Sing heigh, sing ho, the carrion crow,
   Fol de riddle, lol de riddle, hi ding do.

The tailor he shot, but he missed his mark,
   Fol de riddle, lol de riddle, hi ding do,
And shot the old sow quite through the heart;
   Sing heigh, sing ho, the carrion crow,
               Fol de riddle,
                  lol de riddle,
                     hi ding do.

A man of words and not of deeds,
Is like a garden full of weeds;
And when the weeds begin to grow,
It's like a garden full of snow;
And when the snow begins to fall,
It's like a bird upon the wall;
And when the bird away does fly,
It's like an eagle in the sky;
And when the sky begins to roar,
It's like a lion at the door;
And when the door begins to crack,
It's like a stick across your back;
And when your back begins to smart,
It's like a penknife in your heart;
And when your heart begins to bleed,
You're dead, and dead, and dead, indeed.

A frog he would a-wooing go,
    Heigho, says Rowley,
Whether his mother would let him or no.
    With a rowley, powley, gammon
      and spinach,
    Heigho, says Anthony Rowley!

So off he set with his opera hat,
      Heigho, says Rowley,
And on the road he met with a rat.
    With a rowley, powley, gammon
      and spinach,
    Heigho, says Anthony Rowley!

"Pray, Mr. Rat, will you
      go with me,"
Heigho, says Rowley,
"Kind Mrs. Mousey for to
      see?"
With a rowley, powley,
      gammon and spinach,
Heigho, says Anthony Rowley!

When they reached the door of Mousey's
      hall,
                  Heigho, says Rowley,
They gave a loud knock, and they gave a
      loud call,
      With a rowley, powley, gammon
      and spinach,
      Heigho, says Anthony Rowley!

"Pray, Mrs. Mouse, are you within?"
　　　　Heigho, says Rowley,
"Oh, yes, kind sirs, I'm sitting to spin."
　　With a rowley, powley, gammon
　　and spinach,
　　　　Heigho, says Anthony
　　　　　Rowley!

"Pray, Mrs. Mouse, will you give us some
　　beer?
　　　　　Heigho, says Rowley,
For froggy and I are fond of good cheer."
　　With a rowley, powley, gammon
　　and spinach,
Heigho, says Anthony Rowley!

"Pray, Mr. Frog, will you give us a song?
      Heigho, says Rowley,
But let it be something that's not very long."
    With a rowley, powley, gammon
      and spinach,
  Heigho, says Anthony Rowley!

"Indeed, Mrs. Mouse," replied Mr. Frog,
      Heigho, says Rowley,
"A cold has made me as hoarse as a dog,"
    With a rowley, powley, gammon
      and spinach,
  Heigho, says Anthony Rowley!

"Since you have caught cold, Mr. Frog,"
  Mousey said,
      Heigho, says Rowley,

"I'll sing you a song that I have just
    made."
        With a rowley, powley, gammon
            and spinach,
        Heigho, says Anthony Rowley!

But while they were all a merry-making,
            Heigho, says Rowley,
A cat and her kittens came tumbling in.
        With a rowley, powley, gammon
            and spinach,
        Heigho, says Anthony Rowley!

The cat she seized the rat by the crown,
            Heigho, says Rowley,
The kittens they pulled the little mouse down,
        With a rowley, powley, gammon
            and spinach,
        Heigho, says Anthony Rowley!

This put Mr. Frog in a terrible fright;
          Heigho, says Rowley,
He took up his hat, and he wished them
  good-night,
     With a rowley, powley, gammon
       and spinach,
     Heigho, says Anthony Rowley!

But as Froggy was crossing over a brook,
          Heigho, says Rowley,
A lily-white duck came and gobbled
  him up.
     With a rowley, powley, gammon
       and spinach,
     Heigho, says Anthony Rowley!

So there was an end of one, two and
  three,
                Heigho, says Rowley,
The Rat, the Mouse, and the little Frog-gee!
  With a rowley, powley, gammon
    and spinach,
  Heigho, says Anthony Rowley!

A little cock sparrow sat on a green tree,
And he chirruped, he chirruped, so merry
 was he;
A little cock sparrow sat on a green tree,
And he chirruped, he chirruped, so merry
 was he.

A naughty boy came with his wee bow and
 arrow,
Determined to shoot this little cock sparrow,

A naughty boy came with his wee bow and
      arrow,
Determined to shoot this little cock sparrow.

"This little cock sparrow shall make me a
      stew,
And his giblets shall make me a little pie too."
"Oh, no!" said the sparrow, "I won't make
      a stew,"
And he flapped his wings and away he flew!

As I was going to St. Ives,
I met a man with seven wives;
Each wife had seven sacks,
Each sack had seven cats,
Each cat had seven kits;
Kits, cats, sacks, and wives,
How many were going to St. Ives?

A swarm of bees in May
Is worth a load of hay;
A swarm of bees in June
Is worth a silver spoon;
A swarm of bees in July
Is not worth a fly.

Bobby Shaftoe's gone to sea,
Silver buckles on his knee;
He'll come back and marry me,
Bonny Bobby Shaftoe!

Bobby Shaftoe's young and fair,
Combing down his yellow hair,
He's my love for evermore,
Bonny Bobby Shaftoe.

Bryan O'Lin had no breeches to wear,
So he bought him a sheepskin and made
    him a pair.
With the skinny side out, and the woolly
    side in,
"Ah ha, that is warm!" said Bryan O'Lin.

Charley, Charley, stole the barley
    Out of the baker's shop;
The baker came out, and gave him a clout,
    And made poor Charley hop.

Cushy cow bonny,
Let down thy milk,
And I will give thee a gown of silk;
A gown of silk and a silver tee,
If thou wilt let down thy milk to me.

"Croak!" said the Toad, "I'm hungry,
     I think,
To-day I've had nothing to eat or to drink;
I'll crawl to a garden and jump through
     the pales,
And there I'll dine nicely on slugs and
     on snails."

"Ho, ho!" quoth the Frog, "is that what
     you mean?
Then I'll hop away to the next meadow
     stream,
There I will drink, and eat worms and
     slugs too,
And then I shall have a good dinner like
     you."

Doctor Foster went to Glo'ster,
In a shower of rain;
He stepped in a puddle, up to his middle,
And never went there again.

Doctor Faustus was a good man,
He whipped his scholars now and then;
When he whipped them he made them
    dance,
Out of Scotland into France,
Out of France into Spain,
And then he whipped them home again.

Elsie Marley is grown so fine,
She won't get up to serve the swine,
But lies in bed till eight or nine,
And surely she does take her time.

Early to bed, and early to rise,
Makes a man healthy, wealthy and wise.

Every lady in this land
Has twenty nails upon each hand.
Five and twenty on hands and feet.
All this is true without deceit.

Fa, Fe, Fi, Fo, Fum!
I smell the blood of an Englishman:
Be he alive or be he dead,
I'll grind his bones to make me bread.

1   He loves me,
2   He don't!
3   He'll have me,
4   He won't!
5   He would if he could,
6   But he can't,
7   So he don't!

For want of a nail, the shoe was lost,
For want of the shoe, the horse was lost,
For want of the horse, the rider was lost,
For want of the rider, the battle was lost,
For want of the battle, the kingdom was
    lost,
And all from the want of a horseshoe
    nail!

Four and twenty tailors went to kill a
    snail,
The best man among them durs' n't
    touch her tail,
She put out her horns like a little Kyloe
    cow,
Run, tailors, run! or she'll kill you all
    e'en now.

He that would thrive,
Must rise at five;
He that hath thriven,
May lie till seven;
And he that by the plough would thrive,
Himself must either hold or drive.

Higgledy piggledy
    Here we lie,
Pick'd and pluck'd,
    And put in a pie.
My first is snapping, snarling, growling,
My second's industrious, romping and
    prowling.
Higgledy piggledy
    Here we lie,
Pick'd and pluck'd,
    And put in a pie.   *(currant)*

I had four brothers over the sea,
    Perrie, Merrie, Dixie, Dominie.
And they each sent a present unto me,
    Petrum, Partrum, Paradise, Temporie,
    Perrie, Merrie, Dixie, Dominie.

The first sent a chicken, without any
    bones;
The second sent a cherry, without any
    stones.
    Petrum, Partrum, Paradise, Temporie,
    Perrie, Merrie, Dixie, Dominie.

The third sent a book, which no man
    could read;
The fourth sent a blanket, without any
    thread.

Petrum, Partrum, Paradise, Temporie,
Perrie, Merrie, Dixie, Dominie.

How could there be a chicken without
   any bones?
How could there be a cherry without any
   stones?
   Petrum, Partrum, Paradise, Temporie,
   Perrie, Merrie, Dixie, Dominie.

How could there be a book which no
   man could read?
How could there be a blanket without a
   thread?
   Petrum, Partrum, Paradise, Temporie,
   Perrie, Merrie, Dixie, Dominie.

"AS I WAS GOING TO ST. IVES."

"RING A RING O' ROSES."

"THE MAN IN THE WILDERNESS."

"THE FAIR MAID WHO THE FIRST OF MAY"

When the chicken's in the egg-shell,
　　　there are no bones;
When the cherry's in the blossom, there
　　　are no stones.
　　Petrum, Partrum, Paradise, Temporie,
　　Perrie, Merrie, Dixie, Dominie.

When the book's in ye press no man it
　　　can read;
When the wool is on the sheep's back,
　　　there is no thread.
　　Petrum, Partrum, Paradise, Temporie,
　　Perrie, Merrie, Dixie, Dominie.

If you sneeze on a Monday, you sneeze
    for danger;
Sneeze on a Tuesday, kiss a stranger;
Sneeze on a Wednesday, sneeze for a
    letter;
Sneeze on a Thursday, something better;
Sneeze on a Friday, sneeze for sorrow;
Sneeze on a Saturday, see your sweet-
    heart to-morrow.

I love my love with an A, because he's
    Agreeable.
I hate him because he's Avaricious.
He took me to the Sign of the Acorn,
And treated me with Apples.
His name's Andrew,
And he lives at Arlington.
        (*This can be continued through the alphabet*)

If all the seas were one sea,
What a *great* sea it would be!
And if all the trees were one tree,
What a *great* tree it would be!
And if all the axes were one axe,
What a *great* axe that would be!
And if all the men were one man,
What a *great* man he would be!
And if the *great* man took the *great* axe,
And cut down the *great* tree,
And let it fall into the *great* sea,
What a splish splash *that* would be!

I love sixpence, pretty little sixpence,
    I love sixpence better than my life;
I spent a penny of it, I spent another,
    And I took fourpence home to my
        wife.

Oh, my little fourpence, pretty little
        fourpence,
    I love fourpence better than my life;
I spent a penny of it, I spent another,
    And I took twopence home to my
        wife.

Oh, my little twopence, pretty little
        twopence,
    I love twopence better than my life;
I spent a penny of it, I spent another,
    And I took nothing home to my wife.

Oh, my little nothing, my pretty little
    nothing,
   What will nothing buy for my wife?
I have nothing, I spent nothing,
   I love nothing better than my wife.

Eena, deena, dina, du33,
Kattla, weela, wila, wuss,
Spit, spot, must be done,
Twiddlum, twaddlum, twenty-one.
O-U-T spells out!

If I'd as much money as I could spend,
I never would cry old chairs to mend;
Old chairs to mend, old chairs to mend;
I never would cry old chairs to mend.

If I'd as much money as I could tell,
I never would cry old clothes to sell;
Old clothes to sell, old clothes to sell;
I never would cry old clothes to sell.

If ifs and ands
Were pots and pans
There would be no need for tinkers!

If all the world was apple pie,
    And all the sea was ink,
And all the trees were bread and cheese,
    What should we have to drink?

January brings the snow,
Makes our feet and fingers glow.

February brings the rain,
Thaws the frozen lake again.

March brings breezes loud and shrill,
Stirs the dancing daffodil.

April brings the primrose sweet,
Scatters daisies at our feet.

May brings flocks of pretty lambs,
Skipping by their fleecy dams.

June brings tulips, lilies, roses,
Fills the children's hands with posies.

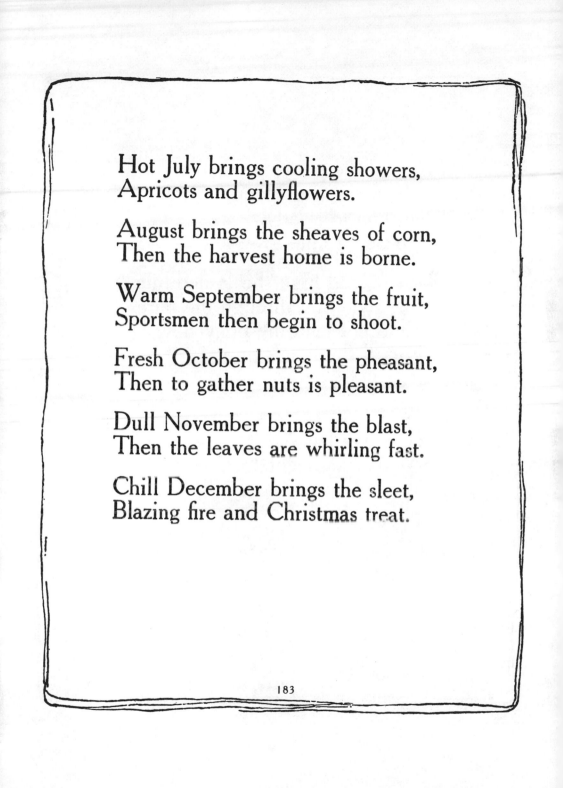

Hot July brings cooling showers,
Apricots and gillyflowers.

August brings the sheaves of corn,
Then the harvest home is borne.

Warm September brings the fruit,
Sportsmen then begin to shoot.

Fresh October brings the pheasant,
Then to gather nuts is pleasant.

Dull November brings the blast,
Then the leaves are whirling fast.

Chill December brings the sleet,
Blazing fire and Christmas treat.

I had a little pony,
  His name was Dapple Grey,
I lent him to a lady,
  To ride a mile away.

She whipped him, she lashed him,
  She rode him through the mire,
I would not lend my pony now,
  For all the lady's hire.

Leg over leg,
As the dog went to Dover;
When he came to a stile,
Jump, he went over.

London Bridge is broken down,
Dance o'er my Lady Lee;
London Bridge is broken down,
With a gay lady.

How shall we build it up again?
Dance o'er my Lady Lee;
How shall we build it up again?
With a gay lady.

Build it up with silver and gold,
Dance o'er my Lady Lee;
Build it up with silver and gold,
With a gay lady.

Silver and gold will be stole away,
Dance o'er my Lady Lee;
Silver and gold will be stole away,
With a gay lady.

Build it up with iron and steel,
Dance o'er my Lady Lee;
Build it up with iron and steel,
With a gay lady.

Iron and steel will bend and bow,
Dance o'er my Lady Lee;
Iron and steel will bend and bow,
With a gay lady.

Build it up with wood and clay,
Dance o'er my Lady Lee;
Build it up with wood and clay,
With a gay lady.

Wood and clay will wash away,
Dance o'er my Lady Lee;
Wood and clay will wash away,
With a gay lady.

Build it up with stone so strong,
Dance o'er my Lady Lee;
Huzza! 'twill last for ages long,
With a gay lady.

My dear, do you know,
How a long time ago,
Two poor little children,
Whose names I don't know,
Were stolen away on a fine summer's
    day,
And left in a wood, as I've heard people
    say.

And when it was night,
So sad was their plight,
The sun it went down,
And the moon gave no light!
They sobbed, and they sighed, and they
    bitterly cried,
And the poor little things, they lay down
    and died.

And when they were dead,
The robins so red
Brought strawberry leaves,
And over them spread;
And all the day long,
They sung them this song:
"Poor babes in the wood! poor babes in
the wood!
And don't you remember the babes in
the wood?"

Mollie, my sister, and I fell out,
And what do you think it was about?
She loved coffee, and I loved tea,
And that was the reason we couldn't
agree.

Monday's bairn is fair of face,
Tuesday's bairn is full of grace,
Wednesday's bairn is full of woe,
Thursday's bairn has far to go,
Friday's bairn is loving and giving,
Saturday's bairn works hard for its living,
But the bairn that is born on the Sabbath
    day
Is bonny and blythe, and good and gay.

    March winds and April showers
    Bring forth May flowers.

Needles and pins, needles and pins,
When a man marries his trouble begins.

Old King Cole
Was a merry old soul,
And a merry old soul was he;
He called for his pipe,
And he called for his bowl,
And he called for his fiddlers three.

Every fiddler, he had a fiddle,
And a very fine fiddle had he;
Twee tweedle dee, tweedle dee, went
    the fiddlers.
Oh, there's none so rare,
As can compare
With King Cole and his fiddlers three!

One misty, moisty morning,
When cloudy was the weather,
There I met an old man
Clothed all in leather;
Clothed all in leather,
With cap under his chin,—
How do you do, and how do you do,
And how do you do again!

Old Mother Goose, when
She wanted to wander,
Would ride through the air
On a very fine gander.

Mother Goose had a house,
'Twas built in the wood,
Where an owl at the door
For sentinel stood.

She had a son Jack,
A plain-looking lad,
He was not very good,
Nor yet very bad.

She sent him to market,
A live goose he bought,
"Here, mother," says he,
"It will not go for nought."

Jack's goose and her gander
Grew very fond;
They'd both eat together,
Or swim in one pond.

Jack found one morning,
As I have been told,
His goose had laid him
An egg of pure gold.

Jack rode to his mother,
The news for to tell,
She called him a good boy,
And said it was well.

Jack sold his gold egg,
To a rogue of a Jew,
Who cheated him out of
The half of his due.

Then Jack went a-courting,
A lady so gay,
As fair as the lily,
And sweet as the May.

The Jew and the Squire
Came behind his back,
And began to belabour
The sides of poor Jack.

But old Mother Goose
That instant came in,
And turned her son Jack
Into famed Harlequin.

She then with her wand,
Touched the lady so fine,
And turned her at once
Into sweet Columbine.

The gold egg into the sea
Was thrown then,—
When Jack jumped in,
And got the egg back again.

The Jew got the goose,
Which he vowed he would kill,
Resolving at once
His pockets to fill.

Jack's mother came in,
And caught the goose soon,
And mounting its back,
Flew up to the moon.

One, two, three, four,
Mary at the cottage door;
Five, six, seven, eight,
Eating cherries off a plate;
O-U-T spells out!

O, the grand old Duke of York,
  He had ten thousand men;
He marched them up a great big hill,
  And he marched them down again!
So when they were up, they were up,
  And when they were down, they were
      down;
And when they were neither down nor up,
  They were neither up nor down.

One, he loves; two, he loves;
Three, he loves, they say;
Four, he loves with all his heart;
Five, he casts away.
Six, he loves; seven, she loves;
Eight, they both love.
Nine, he comes; ten, he tarries;
Eleven, he courts; twelve, he marries.

O the little rusty, dusty, rusty miller!
I'll not change my wife for either gold or
    siller.

Please to remember
The fifth of November,
    Gunpowder treason and plot;
I know no reason
Why gunpowder treason
    Should ever be forgot.

One to make ready,
And two to prepare;
Good luck to the rider,
And away goes the mare.

Pease-pudding hot,
Pease-pudding cold,
Pease-pudding in the pot,
Nine days old.
Some like it hot,
Some like it cold,
Some like it in the pot,
Nine days old.

Peter, Peter, pumpkin-eater,
Had a wife, and couldn't keep her;
He put her in a pumpkin-shell,
And there he kept her very well.

Peter, Peter, pumpkin-eater,
Had another and didn't love her;
Peter learned to read and spell,
And then he loved her very well.

Punch and Judy
    Fought for a pie,
Punch gave Judy
    A knock in the eye.

Says Punch to Judy,
    "Will you have any more?"
Says Judy to Punch,
    "My eyes are too sore."

Poor old Robinson Crusoe!
Poor old Robinson Crusoe!

They made him a coat
Of an old nanny goat,
I wonder how they could do so!
With a ring a ting tang,
And a ring a ting tang,
Poor old Robinson Crusoe!

Robin and Richard were two pretty men;
They lay in bed till the clock struck ten;
Then up starts Robin, and looks at the
    sky,
Oh! brother Richard, the sun's very high:

The bull's in the barn, threshing the corn;
The cock's on the dunghill, blowing his
    horn;
The cat's at the fire, frying of fish,
The dog's in the pantry, breaking his
    dish.

Some little mice sat in a barn to spin,
Pussy passed by, and popped her head in.
"Shall I come in and cut your threads
    off?"
"No, no, kind sir, you'll snap our heads
    off."

Ring a ring o' roses,
A pocketful of posies,
Tisha! tisha!
We all fall down.

See a pin and pick it up,
All the day you'll have good luck;
See a pin and let it lay,
Bad luck you'll have all day.

Solomon Grundy,
Born on Monday,
Christened on Tuesday,
Married on Wednesday,
Took ill on Thursday,
Worse on Friday,
Died on Saturday,
Buried on Sunday;
This is the end
Of Solomon Grundy.

Saw ye aught of my love a-coming from
    the market?
  A peck of meal upon her back,
  A babby in her basket;
Saw ye aught of my love coming from
    the market?

St. Swithin's day, if thou dost rain,
For forty days it will remain;
St. Swithin's day, if thou be fair,
For forty days 'twill rain na mair.

There once were two cats of Kilkenny,
Each thought there was one cat too many,
So they fought and they fit,
And they scratched and they bit,
Till, excepting their nails
And the tips of their tails,
Instead of two cats, there weren't any.

Tit, tat, toe,
My first go,
Three jolly butcher boys
All of a row;
Stick one up,
Stick one down,
Stick one on the old man's crown.

The Lion and the unicorn
Were fighting for the crown;
The Lion beat the unicorn
All round the town.
Some gave them white bread,
And some gave them brown;
Some gave them plum-cake,
And sent them out of town.

There was a fat man of Bombay,
Who was smoking one sunshiny day,
When a bird, called a snipe,
Flew away with his pipe,
Which vexed the fat man of Bombay.

There was a jolly miller
Lived on the river Dee:
He worked and sung from morn till night,
No lark so blithe was he,
And this the burden of his song
For ever used to be—
I jump mejerrime jee!
I care for nobody—no! not I,
Since nobody cares for me.

There was an old woman, as I've heard tell,
She went to market her eggs for to sell;
She went to market all on a market-day,
And she fell asleep on the King's highway.

There came by a pedlar whose name was
    Stout,
He cut her petticoats all around about;
He cut her petticoats up to the knees,
Which made the old woman to shiver and
    freeze.

When this little woman first did wake,
She began to shiver and she began to shake,
She began to wonder and she began to cry,
"Oh! deary, deary me, this is none of I!"

"But if it be I, as I do hope it be,
I've a little dog at home, and he'll know me;
If it be I, he'll wag his little tail,
And if it be not I, he'll loudly bark and
wail."

Home went the little woman all in the dark,
Up got the little dog, and he began to bark;
He began to bark, so she began to cry,
"Oh! deary, deary me, this is none of I!"

There was an old woman called Nothing-
at-all,
Who rejoiced in a dwelling exceedingly
small;
A man stretched his mouth to its utmost
extent,
And down at one gulp house and old
woman went.

There was an old woman tossed up in a
     basket,
Nineteen times as high as the moon;
Where she was going I couldn't but ask it,
For in her hand she carried a broom.

"Old woman, old woman, old woman,"
     quoth I,
Oh whither, oh whither, oh whither so
     high?
"To brush the cobwebs off the sky!"
"Shall I go with thee?" "Aye, by-and-by."

There was a little man,
And he wooed a little maid,
And he said, "Little maid, will you wed,
    wed, wed?
I have little more to say,
Then will you, yea or nay,
For least said is soonest mended-ded,
    ded, ded."

The little maid replied,
Some say a little sighed,
"But what shall we have to eat, eat, eat?
Will the love that you're so rich in
Make a fire in the kitchen?
Or the little god of Love turn the spit,
    spit, spit?"

There's a neat little clock,
  In the schoolroom it stands,
And it points to the time
  With its two little hands.

And may we, like the clock,
  Keep a face clean and bright,
With hands ever ready
  To do what is right.

Twelve pears hanging high,
Twelve knights riding by;
Each knight took a pear,
And yet left eleven there!

There was an old woman, and what do
    you think?
She lived upon nothing but victuals and
    drink:
Victuals and drink were the chief of her
    diet;
Yet this little old woman could never
    keep quiet.

Tell-tale-tit!
Your tongue shall be slit,
And all the dogs in the town
Shall have a little bit.

The man in the wilderness asked me,
How many strawberries grew in the sea?
I answered him, as I thought good,
As many as red herrings grew in the wood.

There was a little man,
And he had a little gun,
And his bullets were made of lead, lead,
    lead.

He went to the brook,
And saw a little duck,
And he shot it right through the head,
    head, head.

He carried it home,
To his old wife Joan,
And bade her a fire to make, make, make.

To roast the little duck,
He had shot in the brook,
And he'd go and fetch her the drake,
    drake, drake.

Three wise men of Gotham,
Went to sea in a bowl;
And if the bowl had been stronger,
My song would have been longer.

Two legs sat upon three legs,
With one leg in his lap;
In comes four legs,
Runs away with one leg.
Up jumps two legs,
Catches up three legs,
Throws it after four legs,
And makes him bring back one leg.

The Queen of Hearts,
She made some tarts,
    All on a summer's day;
The Knave of Hearts,
He stole those tarts,
    And took them clean away.

The King of Hearts
Called for the tarts,
    And beat the Knave full sore;
The Knave of Hearts
Brought back the tarts,
    And vowed he'd steal no more.

Tweedle-dum and Tweedle-dee,
Resolved to have a battle,
For Tweedle-dum said Tweedle-dee
Had spoiled his nice new rattle.

Just then flew by a monstrous crow,
As big as a tar barrel,
Which frightened both the heroes so,
They quite forgot their quarrel.

There was a crooked man, and he went
    a crooked mile,
He found a crooked sixpence against a
    crooked stile;
He bought a crooked cat, which caught
    a crooked mouse,
And they all lived together in a little
    crooked house.

There was a man of Thessaly,
And he was wond'rous wise,
He jump'd into a quickset hedge,
And scratch'd out both his eyes;
But when he saw his eyes were out,
With all his might and main
He jump'd into another hedge,
And scratch'd 'em in again.

Thirty days hath September,
April, June, and November;
February has twenty-eight alone,
All the rest have thirty-one,
Excepting leap-year, that's the time
When February's days are twenty-nine.

Taffy was a Welshman, Taffy was a thief;
Taffy came to my house and stole a piece
    of beef:
I went to Taffy's house, Taffy was not at
    home;
Taffy came to my house and stole a
    marrow-bone.

I went to Taffy's house, Taffy was not in;
Taffy came to my house and stole a silver
    pin;
I went to Taffy's house, Taffy was in bed,
I took up the marrow-bone and flung it at
    his head.

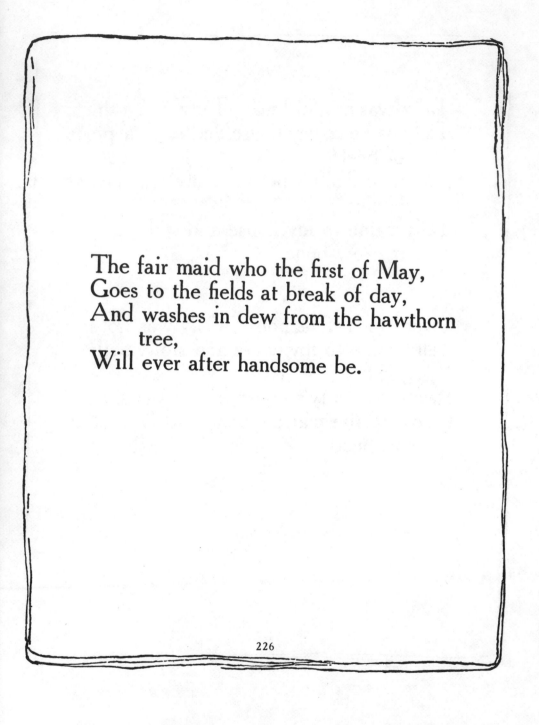

The fair maid who the first of May,
Goes to the fields at break of day,
And washes in dew from the hawthorn
tree,
Will ever after handsome be.

There was a little woman, as I've been
    told,
Who was not very young, not yet very
    old,
Now this little woman her living got,
By selling codlins, hot, hot, hot!

They that wash on Monday,
    Have all the week to dry;
They that wash on Tuesday,
    Are not so much awry;
They that wash on Wednesday,
    Are not so much to blame;
They that wash on Thursday,
    Wash for shame;
They that wash on Friday,
    Wash in need;
And they that wash on Saturday,
    O! they're sluts indeed.

Upon my word and honour,
As I was going to Bonner,
   I met a pig,
   Without a wig,
Upon my word and honour!

When the wind is in the east,
'Tis neither good for man nor beast;
When the wind is in the north,
The skilful fisher goes not forth;
When the wind is in the south,
It blows the bait in the fishes' mouth;
When the wind is in the west,
Then 'tis at the very best.

"Where are you going to, my pretty
    maid?"
"I'm going a-milking, sir," she said.
"May I go with you, my pretty maid?"
"You're kindly welcome, sir," she said.
"What is your father, my pretty maid?"
"My father's a farmer, sir," she said.
"What is your fortune, my pretty maid?"
"My face is my fortune, sir," she said.
"Then I can't marry you, my pretty
    maid!"
"Nobody asked you, sir!" she said.

What care I how black I be,
Twenty pounds will marry me;
If twenty won't, forty shall,
I am my mother's bouncing girl.

When a Twister, a twisting, will twist
    him a twist;
For the twisting of his twist, he three
    times doth intwist;
But if one of the twines of the twist do
    untwist,
The twine that untwisteth, untwisteth the
    twist.

Untwirling the twine that untwisteth between,
He twirls, with the twister, the two in a twine:
Then twice having twisted the twines of the twine,
He twisteth the twine he had twined in twain.

The twain that, in twining, before in the twine,
As twines were untwisted; he now doth untwine:
'Twixt the twain inter-twisting a twine more between,
He, twirling his twister, makes a twist of the twine.

Where have you been all the day,
     My boy, Willy?
"I been all the day
Courting of a lady gay;
But O! she's too young
To be taken from her mammy."

What work can she do,
     My boy, Willy?
Can she bake, and can she brew,
     My boy, Willy?
She can brew, and she can bake,
And she can make our wedding-cake;
But O! she's too young
To be taken from her mammy.

What age may she be?
What age may she be?
     My boy, Willy?
"Twice two, twice seven,
Twice ten, twice eleven;
But O! she's too young
To be taken from her mammy."

When good King Arthur ruled this land,
　　He was a goodly King;
He stole three pecks of barley-meal,
　　To make a bag-pudding.

A bag-pudding the King did make,
　　And stuff'd it well with plums;
And in it put great lumps of fat,
　　As big as my two thumbs.

The King and Queen did eat thereof,
　　And noblemen besides;
And what they could not eat that night,
　　The Queen next morning fried.

When I was a bachelor, I lived by myself,
And all the bread and cheese I got I put
upon a shelf;
The rats and mice did lead me such a life,
That I went to London to get myself a
wife;
The streets were so broad, and the lanes
were so narrow,
I could not get my wife home without a
wheelbarrow.
The wheelbarrow broke, my wife got a
fall,
Down tumbled wheelbarrow, little wife
and all.

Who killed Cock Robin?
"I", said the sparrow,
"With my little bow and arrow,
I killed Cock Robin."

Who saw him die?
"I", said the fly,
"With my little eye,
I saw him die."

Who caught his blood,
"I", said the fish,
"With my little dish,
I caught his blood."

Who'll make his shroud?
"I", said the beetle,
"With my thread and needle,
I'll make his shroud."

Who'll carry the link?
"I", said the linnet,
"I'll come in a minute,
I'll carry the link."

Who'll be the clerk?
"I", said the lark,
"If it's not in the dark,
I'll be the clerk."

Who'll dig his grave?
"I", said the owl,
"With my spade and trowel,
I'll dig his grave."

Who'll be the parson?
"I", said the rook,
"With my little book,
I'll be the parson."

Who'll be chief mourner?
"I", said the dove,
"I mourn for my love,
I'll be chief mourner."

Who'll sing the psalm?
"I", said the thrush,
"As I sit in a bush,
I'll sing the psalm."

Who'll carry his coffin?
"I", said the kite,
"If it's not in the night,
I'll carry the coffin."

Who'll toll the bell?
"I", said the bull,
"Because I can pull,
I'll toll the bell."

All the birds of the air
Fell sighing and sobbing,
When they heard the bell toll
For poor Cock Robin.